ROAD

2

9

18

25

6

CASTLE ST.

HUNTING

CHESTERTON ROAD

VICTORIA ROAD

152
CARDOZO
KINDERSLEY
WORKSHOP

17

G000231616

95

ANGEL COURT
BEGUN – September 1957
FIRST OCCUPIED – October 1959
ARCHITECTS – Husband & Co. (Sheffield)
BUILDERS – J. Youngs & Co. (Norwich)
SENIOR BURSAR – J.R.G. Bradfield
JUNIOR BURSAR – R.H. Glauert

Cutting through the Colleges

KINDERSLEY INSCRIPTIONS
IN CAMBRIDGE UNIVERSITY COLLEGES

Lida Lopes Cardozo Kindersley

AND

Thomas Sherwood

CARDOZO KINDERSLEY · CAMBRIDGE 2010

See page 39 for the finished piece.

CAMBRIDGE UNIVERSITY PRESS
Cambridge, New York, Melbourne, Madrid, Cape Town,
Singapore, São Paulo, Delhi, Dubai and Tokyo

Cambridge University Press
The Edinburgh Building, Cambridge CB2 8RU, UK
www.cambridge.org

First published 2010

Designed by Phil Treble, using the series layout designed
by Eiichi Kono.

Photographs by Philip Moore, Philip Mynott, Eben Sorkin and from
the Cardozo Kindersley Archives.

Map of Cambridge on the inside cover by Oliver Cox.

Small maps by Fiona Boyd.

The book has been set in 12 pt Emilida, a typeface designed by
Lida Lopes Cardozo Kindersley, digitised by ITA Kono Design,
commissioned by Timothy Guy Design for EMI. The typeface was
enhanced in 2010, with many OpenType features and attention to
spacing, by Eben Sorkin.

Every attempt has been made to contact all clients who commissioned
stones that are illustrated here in order to seek their permission.

Printed in the United Kingdom at the University Press, Cambridge

ISBN-13: 978-1-107-00366-8 paperback

Frontispiece: Welsh slate on a parapet of Angel Court, Trinity
College – for more details see page 102.

Contents

Introduction

A couple of years ago Lida asked me to find and photograph every Cardozo Kindersley Workshop inscription at Girton; towards a record which might become a leaflet for College members and visitors. Girton has a large Kindersley store, and not just stones: many oak panels in the chapel, for instance.

This exercise was a useful dry run. The Workshop has carefully organized files of everything that has been done since 1930. Location is simply noted: 'Chapel' is easy enough, but 'Old Chemistry Laboratory' was a challenge. I learnt about inveigling myself into the confidence of college staff, and do not just mean bursars. Porters, gardeners, cleaners proved particularly useful. Colleges change continually with the times; their rooms are remodelled, reassigned, and their old functions forgotten. The Old Chemistry Laboratory turned out to be House Services (but tablet intact).

So when the task was expanded to include all Cambridge colleges, there was some walking and talking to do. It took about a month. My chief experience was of willing and helpful people keen to assist me, after an initial moment of reserve about what I might be up to. In our security-dominated age a strange someone clambering around the place with a camera is apt to arouse suspicion. Quite often concerned college members halted me in my tracks. Only to be pumped for information once I had explained myself.

Colleges vary of course in their Kindersley holdings, from one or two to some 80 brass plates in Trinity College Chapel alone. The locations could be exotic. I enjoyed climbing to the roof parapet where the slate commemorating architects, builders and bursars is exposed to all weather and seen by no-one. The outside wall of a chapel might need quite careful scrutiny to discover the simple initials of a past someone elegantly carved there. 'This room is named...' leans up against some wall on a floor behind a TV set: not in a college building after all now – intentions change. There are plangent stones in college gardens recording people lost, needing leaves and branches to be brushed aside.

And I have been moved, finding the short memories (as I tried to locate this or that forgotten relic) and the lasting beauty of these inscriptions. There is Purcell's Dido's heart-breaking 'Remember me, remember me': Cambridge Kindersley stones make sure we do.

THOMAS SHERWOOD

The book is in two parts:plus a map inside the covers for walks round the colleges. Descriptions of the work in each college are Part I; here the inscriptions are numbered, in red if illustrated. These numbers allow ready reference to Part II; a comprehensive catalogue with dates, materials and dimensions.

Cambridge history of letters

To commission an inscription is a token of personal and public commitment. Inscriptions are given meaning by the people who compose and make them, and by those who read them. And if we look at inscriptions from particular localities or periods, we can learn how people think, and something of what is important to them: what is worth the time, energy and money.

Cambridge is like thousands of places where gravestones and other inscriptions testify to a tradition of commemoration, and street names are essential to finding one's way about. But it is also a place where such tradition is held corporately, and public lettering has to last a long time. This lettering includes shop signs and advertisements. The road to the station has a celebrated, large painted advertisement for Bull's Dairy, readily raising a smile. The dairy has long since

David Kindersley lettering for street names.

closed, but the sign is repainted. So there is an extra dimension, of time. How long do we expect public lettering to last?

Inscriptions are a habit, and a part of memory. They are to be read, and so connect to handwriting and printing. Until the early 16th century nearly all the books in the University's libraries were manuscript, mostly on parchment. And they were made to last. In the mid-16th century, with printed books vastly more common, Cambridge produced a group of people committed to writing in an elegant italic hand, including national names like Roger Ascham and John Cheke. They survive mostly on paper; and they had a strong sense of occasion, of civilised values in shared skills.

Different kinds of lettering for inscriptions of the late 15th and 16th centuries are readily accessible. In King's College chapel we can see the lettera formata on memorial brasses to William Town (1496/7) and John Argentine (1507/8). Other brass lettering there, cut not chased, is in the desk of the lectern for Robert Hacomblen (Provost 1509–28). The windows offer yet different lettering, this time painted. In St John's College chapel

the lettering on the tomb of Hugh Assheton (d.1522) is, unusually, of wrought iron. Skills vary. The accomplished mix of capitals, small capitals and lower case on the monument to Robert Whalley in Queens'

College (1591) chapel is contemporary with disorderly lettering (a 'pleasingly inconsequential local product') for Thomas Lorkyn in Great St Mary's church.

In the 17th century, with changing ecclesiastical moods, more and more stone monuments needed inscription. The proud and large capitals for John Caius (d.1573) and Thomas Legge (1607) in the Gonville & Caius chapel are in striking contrast to much more modest tablets of 1659–61 in St Andrew the Great. Some had just a few words; others ran to a hundred or more. The starkness of the plain capitals for Thomas Buck (d.1669) in

St Edward's church, the various italics in King's College chapel memorials, or the script of the monument to Samuel Sandys (d.1676) in Little St Mary's church speak of exploration in letter shapes as well as very varying skills. Those who cut these brass or stone inscriptions well knew the value of relative letter sizes. The monument to John Smith (d.1715) in St John's College chapel uses three sizes of capitals in two words alone, so as to achieve

JOHANNIS SMITH S.T.P.
LOWTHERIÆ in Agro WESTMARIENSI nati:

the right emphasis. In Trinity College chapel, Isaac Hawkins Browne's monument (1804) is something of a landmark in this history, so-called Egyptian block lettering without serifs.

Inscriptions survive not just on royal coats of arms, but on candelabra, ceilings, organ cases, bells and so on. The great west doors of King's College chapel have Hebrew, carved in wood. The iron-founder's name is seen cast on the 18th century railings ouside the Senate House. But, oddly, it was only in the 20th century that many of the university and college buildings were identified with words. Those by the entrance to the Pitt Building were commissioned from Eric Gill in the 1930s, yet the University Press had been built more than 100 years earlier.

By then, Gill was familiar with Cambridge. The wording on the old medical school in Downing Street (Humphrey Museum 1903), and the raised lettering over the entrance to Westcott House (1904) were among his earliest work. An inscription round the pond at Newnham College (1905) commemorates Henry Sidgwick. The crocodile on the Mond laboratory at the Old Cavendish site (1932) is famous, and there is more to be seen in the Chapel and North Courts of St John's College. The inscription on the Warwick vase in the middle of the Senate House lawn was cut

by Laurie Cribb to his design in about 1933. There is more lettering by Gill in Cambridge than any other place outside London.

This book is about David Kindersley who became Gill's apprentice in 1934, and in 1945 established his own workshop near Cambridge. Encouraged by Brooke Crutchley of the University Press, he moved into Cambridge where he and his work found a ready welcome. The results are to be seen all over the city, in the design of many of the street names, in lettering on public buildings, and in the colleges. In 1986 he married Lida Lopes Cardozo, and since his death in 1995 the tradition has continued under her leadership. The workshop, now in a much extended Victorian school, pursues a steadfast path inspired by Gill so many years ago.

Cambridge draws on these traditions, and more. There is immense variety and subtlety in the wealth of inscriptions to be found in the city, university and colleges: a community committed to care for letters cut – and their wider values.

DAVID McKITTERICK

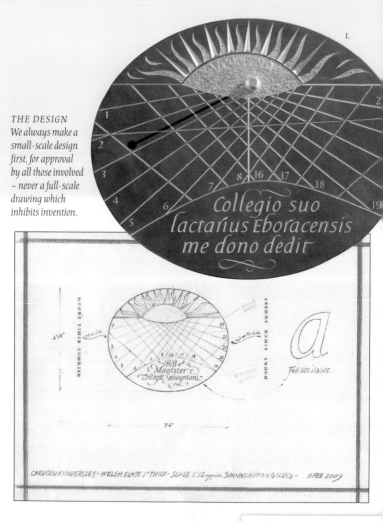

THE DESIGN
We always make a small-scale design first, for approval by all those involved – never a full-scale drawing which inhibits invention.

Collegio suo
lactarius Eboracensis
me dono dedit

CARDOZO KINDERSLEY – WELSH SLATE 1" THICK – SCALE 1:12 approx SUN+INSCRIPTION GILDED – 11 FEB 2009

Once we have the go-ahead, we order the material and shape it. We lay out the lines of the sundial with expert help, and locate the fixing point for the gnomon or nodus to throw its shadow (see Selwyn College section, page 92).

On the making of a sundial

When Selwyn College commissioned a sundial[1] in 2009, we seized the chance (following the dial's Greek inscription – see Selwyn College section, page 92) of documenting each stage for this book. The first thing always is a visit to the proposed site and a meeting with the client. This face-to-face encounter is crucial, and cannot be bypassed by telephone, letters, or e-mail. For any commission, there is more to understand than can be explained. It is about a particular place, and person, and occasion. David Kindersley wrote of a triad of the client-the workshop-the material (from 'Letters Slate Cut', 2004, page 9): 'the workshop should be a living organism and if it isn't its further existence is pointless'.

This meeting is the jump-off point to a first design: having seen and taken in everything, it is home to the drawing board. In the case of a sundial this needs at once the presence of an expert (Dr Frank King here): a sundial is a precision tool that positions us in the universe.

Drawing out the design on the stone with a finely sharpened pencil – always freehand.

THE CUTTING

We have no machinery; the hammer (called the dummy) and chisel are our only tools for this. It is much the longest stage in the making of the stone, and took 5 months here.

14

More cutting: very slowly and very precisely in the disciplined setting of a quiet workshop. You might call it the incisive moment; the work is a mix of exhilaration and huge care.

PAINTING AND GILDING

With the cutting finally done, painting and gilding follow. We flood the letters/lines with paint, for slate is impervious; the surplus is rubbed off later. For gilding, gold leaf is applied to the slate via goldsize (a slow drying varnish).

Rubbing off the excess paint is also the final stage for finishing off the whole surface of the slate, and this is done wet.

We need to rehearse the fitting of the nodus in the workshop.

17

FIXING

We are getting ready for fixing the stone: it is heavy and will need careful handling and protection, including a specially made cover plus plenty of blankets.

How will we manage getting it up on the day? This sketch may look rough, but to the workshop team who are used to working together closely, it is a helpful program of who does what and how on the scaffolding (like a military operation).

An accurate template is essential for siting the holes to be drilled in the wall – all stones have to be spot-on, and a sundial will not work otherwise. Moving from small to larger drills on the wall takes time; back to the precise military operation, which lasted 2 hours here.

The holes are ready, and we hang the stone into them as a dry run. Dr Frank King will now check whether we have got it absolutely right, or need to adjust the position.

It is right, and we are ready to mix the plastic padding which will glue the stone permanently into its new home.

The sundial is up and fixed: we are left to take down the scaffolding and go home in turn.

Part I · The Cambridge colleges

The Workshop.

Christ's College

Whilst the mother of King Henry VII, Lady Margaret Beaufort, was the 1505 foundress of Christ's College, its history as God's-house began 68 years earlier on the present King's College site.

After the Reformation it became a notable Puritan stronghold, with John Milton an altogether appropriate pupil. Another great iconoclast, Charles Darwin, was also here.

At the entrance to 'V' staircase there is a small brass plate on the right (1989), for Dr Sze who lived here.[1] In the Master's Garden a Master's wife is remembered by a 1990 bronze plaque sited by a cherry tree[2]; special permission will be needed for a visit.

The chapel contains a Roll of Honour in wood; the Workshop was involved in correcting one name (1995), and in adding a new name – Douglas Robson (1998).[3]

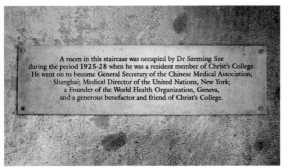

A room in this staircase was occupied by Dr Szeming Sze during the period 1925-28 when he was a resident member of Christ's College. He went on to become General Secretary of the Chinese Medical Association, Shanghai; Medical Director of the United Nations, New York; a Founder of the World Health Organization, Geneva, and a generous benefactor and friend of Christ's College.

1. Letters on brass or bronze can be filled in different colours. Black and white make the highest contrast for legibility. This is particularly important as these metals are unstable and change colour, unless a patina or varnish is applied (both deteriorate in time).

Churchill College

The national and Commonwealth memorial to the great
statesman was founded in 1960. That was followed in 1973
by the Churchill Archives Centre (for his papers). The college
has exceptionally spacious grounds; interestingly its chapel
is tucked away on the periphery just beyond the boundary,
in contrast to the central location expected of Cambridge's
religious foundations.

The western outside wall of the Archives Centre has a huge
'Portland stone' frieze, with inscriptions of donors and of a
Churchill quote carved in situ[1]; this was for the 2002 opening
of a new wing, for Mrs Thatcher's papers. The white stone
is actually reconstituted material rather than Portland;
the Workshop noted this with regret, but admitted 'it cuts

1. Working outside on the wall, well away from the usual comforts of the Workshop:
this is good experience for training – everybody becomes part of the
complete job. Note 'pecking': the inside of the letters is removed with a
point, to leave a rough/smooth contrast with the
fine-rubbed surface of the stone.

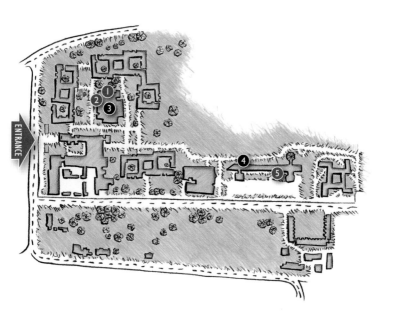

well'. Inside there is a Welsh slate (1989) on the wall of the Jock Colville Hall, for Churchill's private secretary.[2]

The Centre also contains many inscriptions on glass panels (2002 & 2008)[3]; they can be seen on the way from the ground floor, up the stairs and on the first floor. There are directions, the names of the Centre, of the Stephen Roskill Library, and panels of benefactors. Another glass etching details the contents of a display case, with flags from the Falklands conflict.

Two more (real) Portland stone inscriptions record foundation and opening of the Maersk Mc-Kinney Moller Building. The foundation stone (1991) is set into the outside western aspect, to the left of a flight of stone steps.[4] The opening by the Queen of Denmark is celebrated by the 1992 stone inside the entrance lobby on the right.[5]

THE JOCK COLVILLE
HALL
named in recognition of
SIR JOHN COLVILLE
CB CVO
1915 – 1987
Diplomat · Banker · Writer
Principal Private Secretary
to Sir Winston Churchill
Honorary Fellow
of the College
For his service to the
foundation and life of
Churchill College

2. Welsh slate, letters inlaid with gold leaf.

5. Note ligatures binding H & E (twice) and U & E, also 'nesting' where letters tuck into one another (all in lines 1 & 3).

HER MAJESTY QUEEN INGRID OF DENMARK
INAUGURATED THIS BUILDING
THE MAERSK McKINNEY MØLLER CENTRE
FOR CONTINUING EDUCATION
ON THE 2ND OF OCTOBER 1992

Clare College

The second oldest Cambridge college was founded in 1326, though the endowment naming it only came a few years later from Lady Elizabeth de Clare. It was in fact 'Clare Hall' till 1856. The present elegant buildings date from the mid 17th century onwards.

In the ante-chapel (right) there is a 1950 walnut War Memorial case with Hopton Wood stone corbels, inscribed '1939–1945 In Memoriam'.[1] In the chapel itself, look for a touching 2006 brass plate, bent round the base of a candle-holder: the tragic early death of a Choral Scholar.[2] It is in the rear row of the south choir stalls.

2. Lettering was engraved on the flat, before wrapping the brass around the base of the candle-holder.

1.

The wall under the west archway, toward the bridge, has a Ketton stone inscription from 2000 for Paul Mellon, a benefactor who lived in the college 70 years before.[3]

There is also a 2008 brass plaque naming the head-and-shoulders sculpture of Sir David Attenborough[4]; it is reached down some steps to the Buttery through the 'H' entrance.

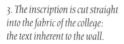

4. Great attention is paid to spacing, however simple the text.

3. The inscription is cut straight into the fabric of the college: the text inherent to the wall.

Clare Hall

The expansion of research in Cambridge after WWII led to a large number of new graduates and senior academics that put the established colleges under

strain. The founding of Clare Hall in 1966 was a timely response, reviving the former name of Clare College. Since then Clare Hall has seen considerable development westwards in Herschel Road.

The college has 7 Welsh slate plaques naming its houses. They began with the Brian Pippard (1997)[1] and Leslie Barnett (1999)[2] Buildings; then Gillian Beer[3], Paul Mellon[4], Robert Honeycombe[5], Michael Stoker[6] and Anthony Low (2000).[7] The last is a stone of interesting vertical design, in harmony with the tiles lining this outside wall.

7.

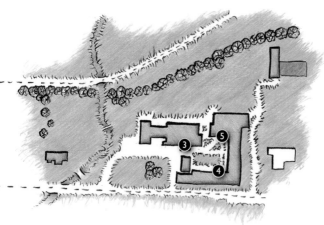

2.

All the nameplates are of Welsh slate, with the letters painted off-white for clarity – these are really street signs for the separate houses.

33

10. The three inches thick Portland stone is in the ground – a serious alternative to a brass plaque at the base of the tree.

A 1997 statue between the Barnett and Pippard Buildings, inscribed for Libby Gardner, has 4 Welsh slate slabs as a square round the plinth.[8] Another open-air Welsh slate stone, from 2008, is itself sculptural; it commemorates Sanae Asahara, near the Ashby Library.[9]

Close by there is a circular Portland stone in the lawn round a tree, for John Arthur Garrod: 'VBI CARITAS ET AMOR, DEVS IBI EST' – Where charity and love are, God is there (1997).[10]

9. Even though this is a solid standing stone, the hole giv an extra perspective of light. Note the always elongated S derived from the start to her first name.

IN MEMORY OF
SANAE
ASAHARA
1948-2006
VISITING FELLOW
1988-1989
FROM HER HUSBAND
BRUCE
EASTWOOD
VISITING FELLOW
1989

Corpus Christi College

A highly unusual foundation in 1352: by two guilds of townspeople, rather than by the nobility. That did not stop traditional Cambridge town versus gown battles; 30 years later irate citizens stormed the college, incensed over rents.

In the ante-chapel, on the right, a 1978 brass tablet records gratitude to the American Friends of Cambridge University, 'in special memory of Sir George Thomson'.[1]

2. The large italic letters are cut straight into the new wall, and painted red.

The new Taylor Library is named on its outside stone wall by a 2008 inscription cut in situ.[2] Opposite in the same Library courtyard are 'T', 'X', 'Y' and a disabled sign cut into the stone above that building's entrances.[3]

3.

Inside, the library has a stunning 2007 glass window in four panels, with quotations of special Corpus interest.[4]

...LEGANDA ANNORUM
ESTENIMISSVORVM
...PHORM

WHAT A WORLD
OF PROFITE AND
DELIGHT
OF POWER OF
HONOVR AND
OMNIPOTENCE
IS PROMISED TO
THE STVDIOVS
ARTIZAN
dar pidely deronme
danabocapyycon
rondaindellie
heohananinpinc
onsefannemeanon

In Latin at the top 'the pelican is greatly devoted to its chicks'; at the bottom, in medieval characters, King Alfred laments 'They had little benefit from these books, for they could not understand anything of them' (so he translated them). The central quote from Christopher Marlowe's Faustus is in clear English (and Doctor Faustus could have been written whilst the playwright was at the college):

> O what a world of profite and delight
> Of power, of honor, and omnipotence
> Is promis'd to the Studious Artizan!

The Dr John Taylor of the library is also the inventor of the remarkable Corpus clock at the north-west corner of the college site, facing King's Parade. The Bath stone at the base says in medieval Latin: The world and its desires pass away.[5] A second edition of this 2008 piece can be seen inside the library at present – actually the first go on mistaken dimensions for the clock site!

The library has two more stones. On an Ancaster stone (2007) in the floor the names of John N. Insall & Michael A. R. Freeman are inscribed, for contributions to medicine.[6] GIRDLERS' ROOM is high up on a wall, a 2008 Welsh slate.[7]

5. The Latin tradition of indicating the missing N by a stroke over the preceding vowel: straight from the college's old Parker Library, housing a remarkable collection of medieval books.

10. *The college's pelican in its piety.*

Bookcases in the library show 27 wooden blocks of various capital letters for the shelves; and a further 12 record 'This section was funded by the students of...'.[8] The Workshop also designed letterheads for the Librarian's stationery.[9]

An excursion to the churchyard of St. Andrew & St. Mary in Grantchester: a place long linked with the college. In 1950 David Kindersley carved a Portland stone pelican on top of a column which is a memorial to Corpus Fellows[10]; this bird is a recurring college motif, mirrored in front on the 2006 green slate gravestone for Michael McCrum, a past Master.[11]

8.

11.

39

The plaque reads:

TO COMMEMORATE THE FOUNDATION IN 1964 OF
DARWIN COLLEGE
BY GONVILLE AND CAIUS COLLEGE
ST. JOHN'S COLLEGE AND TRINITY COLLEGE
IN THE UNIVERSITY OF CAMBRIDGE

Darwin College

This graduate college dates from 1964 when Gonville & Caius, St John's and Trinity Colleges founded it as a joint venture. The great Charles Darwin's second son, Sir George Darwin, was Plumian Professor of Astronomy in the University, and had bought Newnham Grange in 1885. The chance arose in 1963 to acquire this house as the starting core for the new college.

The 1969 Foundation stone (Portland) in the entrance hall therefore bears four coats of arms: the three founding colleges' first, and last the new Darwin's.[1] In the curious language of heraldry, Darwin is characterised by 'three escallops or'.

1. Three people worked on this large stone at the same time, carving away the interior to leave the shield shapes standing proud. This heraldry is fully painted and gilded using an oil-based signwriter's paint. The letters were v-cut into the sunken panel.

Downing College

Founded in 1800, only half of the intended design of this college with its spacious grounds was completed; accounting for the missing half, known as the Downing site, now being a large science/laboratory block for the University.

The Ante-Chapel has a Welsh slate of 2007 for a remarkable man, Stephen Fleet.[1] He was first the College's Bursar, and then became the University's Registrary 1983–97. The Mastership of his college capped a fine Cambridge career.

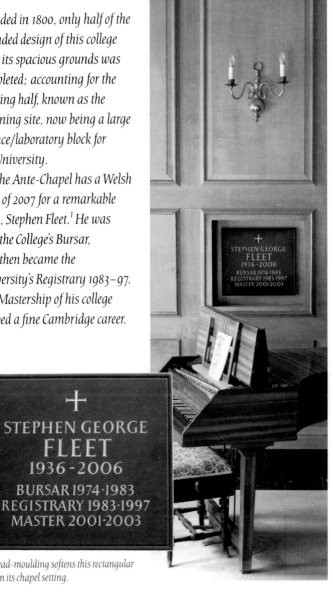

✝

STEPHEN GEORGE
FLEET
1936-2006

BURSAR 1974-1983
REGISTRARY 1983-1997
MASTER 2001-2003

1. A bead-moulding softens this rectangular slate in its chapel setting.

Emmanuel College

The college is a 1584 foundation on the site of an old Dominican priory; but Queen Elizabeth's Chancellor of the Exchequer, Sir Walter Mildmay, was a Puritan who intended his college for educating Protestant preachers. Mildmay and the first Master were at pains though to make clear that they were not bent on separatism or dissension.

The new Queen's Building by Michael and Patty Hopkins (with some echoes of their Glyndebourne opera house) had its Ketton Foundation stone laid in 1993 on the South wall.[1] The Queen came to open the building in 1995; two Italian slates inside the entrance were commissioned for the event.[2 & 3]

THIS FOUNDATION STON
WAS LAID BY
HER ROYAL HIGHNES
THE PRINCESS OF WAL
IN THE YEAR OF OUR LORD 19
ON THURSDAY NOVEMBER
LORD ST JOHN OF FAWSLI
BEING MASTER

1. *Ketton stone is a great building stone and lasts amazingly, but it is open and soft, so a very sharp chisel is used, like that of a woodcarver.*

THE QUEEN'S BUILDING
DESIGNED BY MICHAEL AND PATTY HOPKINS
WAS OPENED BY
HER MAJESTY THE QUEEN
ON WEDNESDAY 19 APRIL 1995

2.

3.

r · J·Brown · C·Burgoyne · P·Burke · A·
nan · A·Cramp · Y·Cripps · D·Cupitt · (
e · R·Gray · M·Gross · L·Hall · C·Hardc
Lane · F·Leeper · D·Livesey · S·Marks · R·

2 & 3. All the College Fellows were named on this stone.

The letters were stained in the darker colour inherent to Ketton stone.

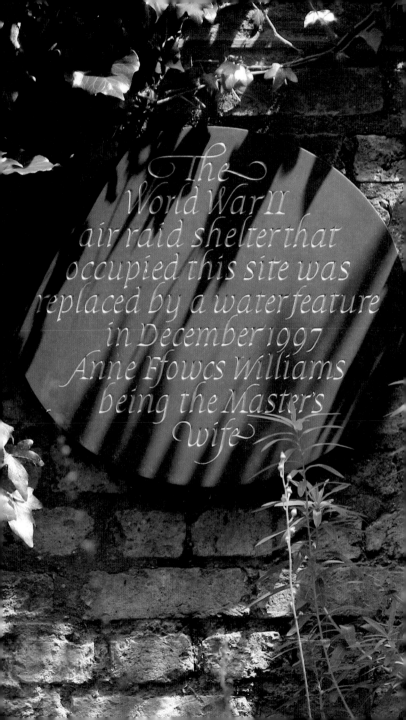

The
World War II
air raid shelter that
occupied this site was
replaced by a water feature
in December 1997
Anne Ffowcs Williams
being the Master's
wife

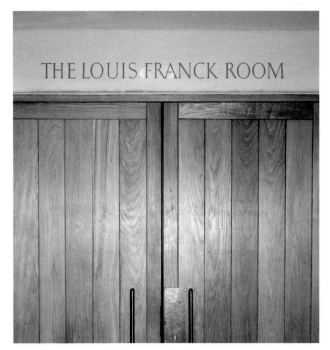

5. *Letters cut straight into plaster, again with a woodcarving chisel*

The building also had its Isobel & Kirby Laing[4] and Louis Franck[5] Rooms named that year: inscriptions cut directly into polished plaster and painted blue.

The Master's Garden is not open to the public; the illustration here is of its 2002 Welsh slate roundel, documenting interesting local history, from air raids to water idyll.[6]

). *Italic, or cursive, letters derive from the rhythm and flow of the running hand: an apt letter form for the message here.*

Fitzwilliam College

Fitzwilliam House began in 1869 as a non-collegiate foundation for undergraduates who wanted to study in Cambridge but were too poor to enter a college. It became a college itself in 1966 – the grant system had done away with the original purpose.

In the courtyard of Wilson House there is a 1993 Portland Foundation stone on the outside wall, for F. Peter Wilson, the architects and contractors.[1] In the same south-west area of the grounds stands a statue of the first 1869 undergraduate; a Welsh slate on the plinth records its 1995 unveiling.[2]

1. Note the ligatures in the top line, binding the U & N and N & E, to give the whole inscription an even rhythm whilst allowing the letters to be of good size. For outdoor inscriptions a good depth of letters is necessary to make them last.

THE FIRST
UNDERGRADUATE
1869
UNVEILED BY
H·R·H·PRINCE PHILIP
CHANCELLOR
OF THE UNIVERSITY
VISITOR
OF THE COLLEGE
TO CELEBRATE
125 YEARS OF
FITZWILLIAM
14 JUNE 1995

*This statue
the generous donation of
Professor N·G·POUNDS
is by Christopher Marvell*

Girton College

The first Cambridge women's college began in 1869 at Hitchin,
Hertfordshire, 3 years after Miss Emily Davies, a Victorian
dynamo, had started a public subscription scheme for women's
higher education. She sounded both London and Cambridge
Universities at first: their tutors visited to teach at Hitchin.
But in 1872 the Girton site was purchased (safely 2 miles out
of town), with a move there the next year. Cambridge degrees
for women still continued on an 'as-if' basis for decades until
full University membership in 1948. Men joined the college
in 1977.

 Girton is unique in having a large collection of wood
inscriptions carved directly into the oak panels lining the Chapel

1.

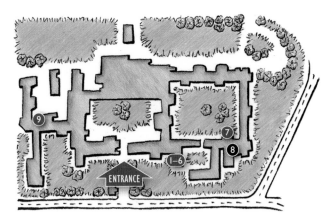

stalls and walls. They commemorate past Fellows;
from 1952 to 1978 David Kindersley added 41 inscriptions.[1]
Of these 16 are individual panels, and 25 are names added
to the large composite boards (east end). Two of the individual
series are illustrated.

ETHEL SOPHIA FEGAN
1877–1975
STUDENT 1896–1900, RESEARCH FELLOW
1935–37, LIBRARIAN AND REGISTRAR OF
THE POLL 1928–30. HON. FELLOW 1948–75
NIL ACTUM CREDENS DUM QUID
SUPERESSET AGENDUM

At the west end of the chapel there are 5 stones for past Mistresses. They begin in 1952 with Kathleen Teresa Blake Butler [2] (Welsh slate with Caen stone mouldings and Portland stone corbels); then Katharine Jex-Blake [3] (1952, Portland stone with marble capping); Edith Helen Major [4] (1952, Portland stone with Black Hopton Wood stone capping); Helen Marion Wodehouse [5] (1965, Nabresina marble); finally Mary Cartwright [6] (2003, Jerusalem Gold limestone).

6. Lettering going round the edge, framing the biographical details,
for a pithy summary to embrace the individual and her work.

AN EMINENT MATHEMATICIAN

MARY LUCY CARTWRIGHT
DBE · MA(Oxon) · DPhil · ScD · FRS
17 December 1900 - 3 April 1998

Mistress of the College 1949-1968
Fellow 1930-1949 & 1968-1998
Director of Studies in Mathematics 1936-1948
University Lecturer in Mathematics 1935-1959
Reader in the Theory of Functions 1959-1968
Honorary Fellow of St Hugh's College, Oxford

A SINGLE-MINDED SEARCH FOR TRUTH

WHOSE PIONEERING WORK · FORMS THE BASIS OF CHAOS THEORY · ON NON-LINEAR DIFFERENTIAL EQUATIONS

3.

5.

7. *This panel was part of the building. David Kindersley entered into the spirit of its feel and size by cutting away the interior background to leave the letters raised – note the playful OF and ligatured H & E to keep this line in symmetry.*

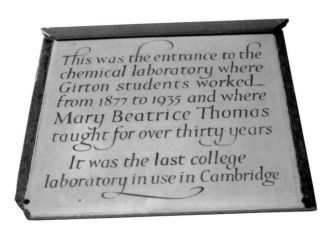

This was the entrance to the
chemical laboratory where
Girton students worked
from 1877 to 1935 and where
Mary Beatrice Thomas
taught for over thirty years
It was the last college
laboratory in use in Cambridge

*9. The only example left in Cambridge of signwriting by the
Workshop, painted with a brush on a prepared piece of plywood.*

The Library's outside east wall in Woodlands Court has a large
1969 carving, cut in situ into an existing tablet of Darley Dale
stone. It commemorates Thomas McMorran as benefactor.[7]
Inside the Library Annexe there is a celebratory oak tablet
upstairs, given by the Librarian Helen Isabelle McMorran,
also 1969.[8]

The least imposing and most charming piece is a tiny paint-
and-plywood tablet of 1956 for the once Chemical Laboratory.[9]
It needs sharp eyes: follow the ground floor corridors northwards
from the Porter's Lodge; the white tablet appears half-way down
the last corridor opposite Ash Court, on the right above a door.

Gonville & Caius College

Gonville's foundation was 1348,
with refounding in 1557 by
Dr Caius. He was really
John Keys, but italianized
his name through studying
and practising medicine in
Padua (though still with English
pronunciation).

*THIS
FOUNDATION STONE
WAS LAID BY
NEIL McKENDRICK
MASTER OF
GONVILLE & CAIUS
COLLEGE
18TH JUNE
2005*

1.

The Kindersley work is in West Road, for
new buildings there next to Harvey Court. The 2005 Foundation
Stone is in the floor of the (right-hand) entrance lobby of the
accommodation block[1]: a fine Ancaster Hard White stone best
viewed by climbing the staircase above. The Stephen Hawking
Building has the 2008 opening by the Duke of Edinburgh
commemorated in the outside floor of the entrance, cut in situ[2];
the adjacent wall on the right has additional letters cut for the
builders and architects.[3]

2. This long horizontal inscription is cut with the insides
of the letters flat (as opposed to the more usual v-cut),
so walking on them is no problem. In time dirt will settle on
the rough-pecked letters, making them clearer by contrast.

THIS·BUILDING·WAS·OPENED·BY·H

CHANCELLOR·OF·THE·UNIVERSITY·17

DUKE·OF·EDINBURGH·KG·KT·CHANCE

2007

THIS BUILDING
WAS OPENED BY
HER MAJESTY
QUEEN ELIZABETH
THE QUEEN MOTHER
29 MAY 1957

2.

Homerton College

Long history for a comparatively recent Cambridge college: in 1730 the King's Head Society was founded by 'a few Protestant Dissenters' in London, for the education of young men entering the Congregational Church. Homerton High Street in the East End became its home that century; in the 19th its function changed to training men and women teachers. The move to Cambridge occurred in 1894, and meant another change: women only. Men were again admitted from the 1970s.

In 1957 the college coat of arms was carved in Ketton stone over the then entrance, now to the north of the new main entrance buildings.[1] The college wanted the arms coloured; David Kindersley successfully resisted this, arguing that the carving would become isolated from the rather matt building. Also outside, to its left and from the same year, there is the Ketton stone celebrating the building's opening by Queen Elizabeth the Queen Mother.[2]

Facing the Hills Road entrance drive there is a double Portland stone (1973) saying 'Homerton College' twice at right angles[3]; it was moved from the original entrance site.

3. David Kindersley's street-lettering (seen all over Britain and the Commonwealth as well as Cambridge) prizes clarity and legibility; classic elegance with perfect spacing is part of this stone's street cred.

Hughes Hall

The 'Cambridge Training College', founded in 1885 to train
women teachers, marks the beginning of the oldest graduate
college in Cambridge. The first Principal, Miss Hughes, told a
Royal Commission in 1894 'we shall never get first-rate training
until men and women are trained together'.

The success of the college in educational innovation has
been reflected in its building program: a Welsh slate inside
a new hall of residence on the Fenner's site commemorates the
2005 opening.[1]

THIS BUILDING WAS OPENED ON 28 APRIL 2005 BY SIR PETER MANSFIELD NOBEL LAUR.

1. As these letters can only
be seen from below we used
an elongated form for
them: classic in
proportions but without
serifs – in keeping with the
building's modern
architecture. Some letters
'nest' into another's space
(like the L & D) or are
ligatures (W & A have
become one character).

58

Jesus College

Founded in 1496 by John Alcock, Bishop of Ely, the college retains a cockerel as its motif. Both a cock and eagle can be seen carved on the 1973 oak memorial doors leading to the Hall stairs.[1] In the Hall itself there are 14 corbels reaching to the ceiling, all repainted and regilded in 1972[2]; the college thanked the Workshop 'for bringing out the little features such as owls and snails'. In the cloisters past the oak doors (eastern wall) is the 1961 Latin slab for William Welsh in Nabresina marble[3] ('one of the best pieces of

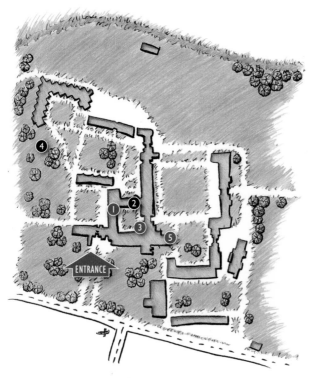

Nabresina that I have ever seen' wrote David Kindersley). One of the many sculptures in the college grounds is Mortal Man, with a Westmorland green slate inscription on its plinth (1967).[4]

The outside east wall of the Chapel (north end) has a terse and touching 1969 carving of initials on it: 'FB 1893–1969'.[5] This is the same Dr Frederick Brittain as on the oak memorial doors.

1. David Kindersley wrote to the college: 'I suggest having the cock and eagle in what amounts to one-inch relief whereas the subsidiary matter such as leaves and sun rays will be in half-inch relief'.

King's College

Cambridge's greatest building, the College Chapel, was begun in 1446, 5 years after the college's foundation. But the work faltered on Henry VI's death, and was not completed till a century (and several Kings) later, with Henry VIII on the throne.

In room P, off the southern interior of the ante-chapel, there is a 1950 Welsh slate on the north wall, in memory of Herbert William Richmond.[1] His family, commissioning the stone, wrote with delight at 'simple design and beautiful lettering'.

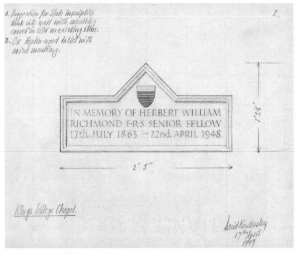

1. David Kindersley's initial design shows how he echoed the pattern of the leaded glass above the stone – this was not taken up. Designs are kept fluid, and changes are made right up to the last chisel blow. This slate is sunk into the existing masonry; double-beaded moulding top and sides (single at the bottom) ties it in gently (compare with Downing College on page 41).

IN MEMORY OF
HERBERT WILLIAM
RICHMOND F.R.S.
SENIOR FELLOW
BORN 17th JULY 1863
DIED 22nd APRIL 1948

Lucy Cavendish College

Founded in 1965 for the specific advancement of women's education, the college had its beginnings in the 1950s as 'The Dining Group' of concerned Cambridge women academics. Its prolific building program since includes Warburton Hall (on the left via the entrance drive). The 1993 Portland stone on the outside left here commemorates the opening by a former Cambridge student, Queen Margrethe of Denmark.[1]

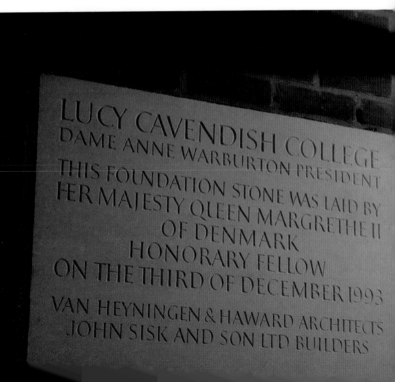

LUCY CAVENDISH COLLEGE
DAME ANNE WARBURTON PRESIDENT
THIS FOUNDATION STONE WAS LAID BY
HER MAJESTY QUEEN MARGRETHE II
OF DENMARK
HONORARY FELLOW
ON THE THIRD OF DECEMBER 1993
VAN HEYNINGEN & HAWARD ARCHITECTS
JOHN SISK AND SON LTD BUILDERS

1. *The rough drawing-out of the design onto the stone allows us to plan the work as we go – in the search for the ideal of how the best possible piece can be wrought. That is why we never make a full size design for the client.*

Magdalene College

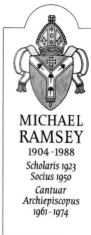

'Monks' Hostel' for Benedictine student-monks was the beginning of this college in 1421. It is said that the north-of-the-river site was to distance the place from the temptations of the town. By the 1470s there was a new patron, and it became 'Buckingham College'. Refounded as 'Magdalene College' in 1542 by Lord Audley, its odd pronunciation Maudlyn may have had something to do with the new founder's conceit: early documents say 'Maudleyn' (incorporating his name).

MICHAEL RAMSEY

1904-1988

Scholaris 1923
Socius 1950

Cantuar Archiepiscopus
1961-1974

3. The full colours for the heraldry are inlaid with enamel paint.

Cambridge Kindersley work may sometimes be thought of as just commemorating the great and good; but modest remembrances are there too, and particularly touching. In the bar, once the Junior Common Room, there is an inscription over the fireplace from 1967, for an undergaduate dying in 1965. 'Through the generosity of Mr & Mrs Alastair Thomson the remaking of this room was completed in 1966 in memory of their son Nigel'.[1]

The Chapel has a number of brass plates: e.g. in the stalls from 2002 for Robert Latham, editor of Pepys' Diary[2], and 2004/6 for the Ramseys. Michael Ramsey was the Archbishop of Canterbury; his plate in the choir stalls north has the Canterbury heraldry on it[3]; and his father Arthur is next door,

2.

...GH THE GENEROSITY OF MR & MRS ALASTAIR THOMSON THE REMAKING
...HIS ROOM WAS COMPLETED IN 1966 IN MEMORY OF THEIR SON NIGEL

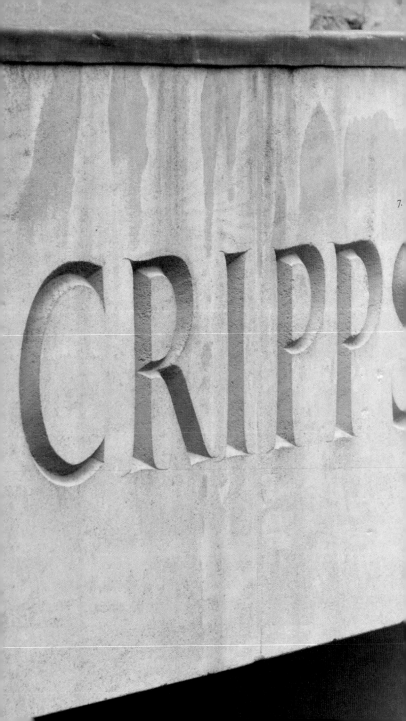

a plain plate for the Director of Studies in Mathematics and President.[4] There is also a larger 2006 brass for 6 Presidents with a redesigned college coat of arms (Presidential stalls west).[5] The benefactors of the Goetze & Gwynn organ are commemorated in the ante-chapel with a 2001 plate[6] (the terse Workshop memo for the letters reads: 'not Cambridge blue – real proper blue')

Cripps Court (in Chesterton Lane) has carvings in situ on the front outside: the Cripps Court title[7] and the handsome College 'Garde ta foy' motto[8] (this is 'Keep faith', not 'watch your liver'). Inside in the entrance lobbies there are two Welsh slates: the foundation and opening stones, all 2005. [9 & 10]

The foundation stone of this court
was laid by
EDWARD AND ROBERT CRIPPS
Benefactors of Magdalene College
20 May 2004

NON OMNIS MORIAR

9. 'One of the great delights of cutting into slate is that the chisel leaves the cut white, in marked contrast with the dark surface. Therefore every cut shows, even the finest hairline. The revelation of this white plane thrills the lettercutter and goads him on to do his best work, right through to the final point, cut or flourish of his intended design. It is certain that in the right hands nothing cuts more finely than blue-black slate' (David Kindersley).

Presented by
HARRY WILKINSON
in memory of his wife
ELIZA *née* ANGEL
1879 - 1949
May those who study here attain like
her a well trained hand and mind

1. As at Girton College, the smallest pieces can be the most fetching – note the delicate leaves. The 'well trained hand and mind' ring loud bells for the Workshop's tradition.

Murray Edwards College

New Hall began in 1954 as the third women's undergraduate college in Cambridge. Its renaming honours its Founder President and generous donors.

The 1957 Wilkinson brass plate is set into the top of a large oak table at the far end of the Dame Rosemary Murray Library (ask at the Porters' Desk).[1]

Newnham College

Cambridge's second women's undergraduate college opened in 1871. It has extensive grounds and in these stands a sinuous sculpture 'Swimming' by Ralph Brown (directions from the Porters' Desk). The 1965 Welsh slate on the plinth records it as the gift of Julia Pleister, in memory of her friend Edith Marjorie Martland – Croix de Guerre (avec palme), Surgeon & Pathologist – i.e. World War I and a singular woman pioneer.[1]

1. *Even on first taking down the wording of the long inscription, David Kindersley was already preparing a design on the spot. The immediacy of the first meeting with a client, a text or a site for the work are important elements in shaping the outcome.*

Pembroke College

Mary de St Pol, the widow of the Earl of Pembroke, was the foundress of the college in 1347. A royalist Ely bishop, imprisoned in the Tower during the Civil War, vowed to build a new chapel if he were released. That happened, and his young nephew was to hand as a budding architect: the Chapel is the first work of Christopher Wren.

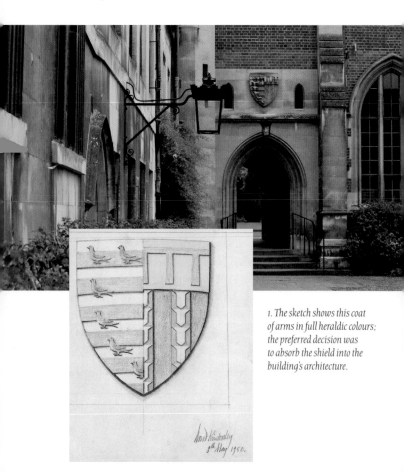

1. The sketch shows this coat of arms in full heraldic colours; the preferred decision was to absorb the shield into the building's architecture.

Straight on from the gates, above the entrance to the Screens
Passage, the college coat of arms was carved in 1950 (Clipsham
stone); the birds are 'an orle of martlets' from the Pembrokes.[1]
1952 saw the restoration (recutting and colouring) of a
long Latin inscription beginning SISTE TE PAULUM
on the slate at the entrance to the Old Library[2] (opposite
Porters' Lodge).

Two bookplates were designed
in 1971 for a Master and his
wife, Sydney Castle Roberts[3] and
Marjorie Roberts.

The college commissioned
engravings of silverware (not
on view) between 1977–81[4]
– a quaich is a shallow cup, from
the Gaelic cuach.

4.

The 1998 sundial on the south of the new Master's Lodge, seen in Tennis Court Road, was cut into stone in situ, and is spectacular.[5] Note equation-of-time panel below, to convert dial time to clock time; much careful research was needed for this.

5. *A ready advantage of working for Cambridge University is finding an expert for nearly everything. Our accurate calibration of the sundial came from Dr Frank King, seen here holding the bottom of the ruler for setting out the time-lines.*

Peterhouse

*A unique place in Cambridge history: it is the oldest college,
founded in 1284 by an Ely bishop, Hugo de Balsham.*

IN MEMORIAM RICARDI HENRICI LOVELOCK
LEE *is the beginning of the 1957 inscription carved into
an external Ketton stone wall backing the New Kitchen (south).[1]
The asymmetrical lay-out was influenced by the vertical joints
of the stone courses. In the Deer Park beyond, hidden under trees,
there is a moving 1998 York stone on the ground: a memorial to
a child lost, it is simply named 'DG'.[2]*

*The 1984 Ward Library is celebrated by a Cumbrian green
slate in the entrance hall.[3] Two grand columns inside have a*

HANC BIBLIOTHECAM
DOMVS SANCTI PETRI
ALVMNORVM SOCIORVM AMICORVM MVNIFICENTIA
IN MVSAEO OLIM ARCHAEOLOGICO INSTRVCTAM
SOLLEMNITER INAVGVRAVIT
PETRVS EPISCOPVS ELIENSIS
COLLEGII VISITATOR ET FVNDATORIS SVCCESSOR
DIE VII MENSIS IVLII ANNO SALVTIS MCMLXXXIV
FVNDATIONIS DCC

3. *The shape and material for this inscription were much determined
by the lambent setting on an elongated library wall.*

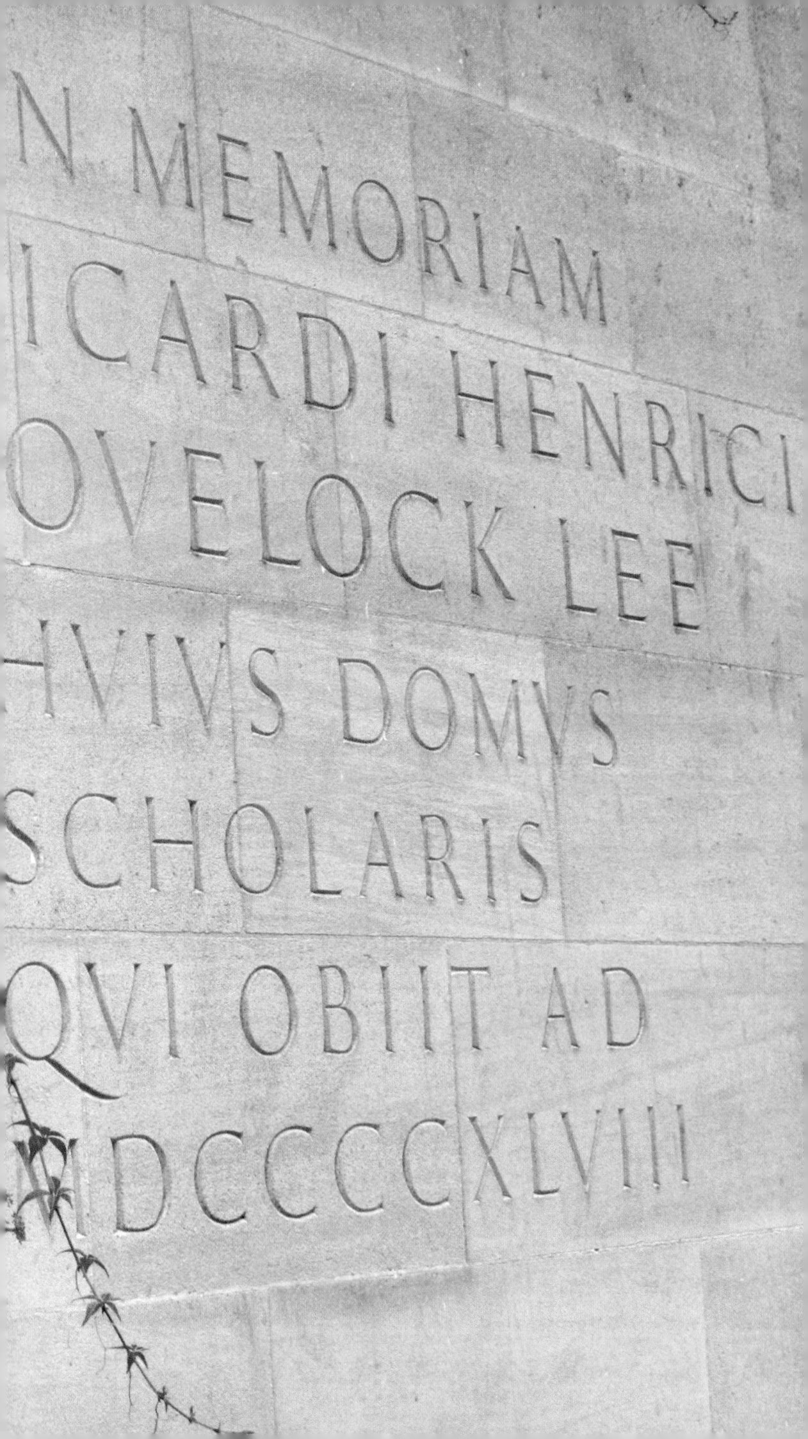

N MEMORIAM
ICARDI HENRICI
OVELOCK LEE
HVIVS DOMVS
SCHOLARIS
QVI OBIIT AD
DCCCCXLVIII

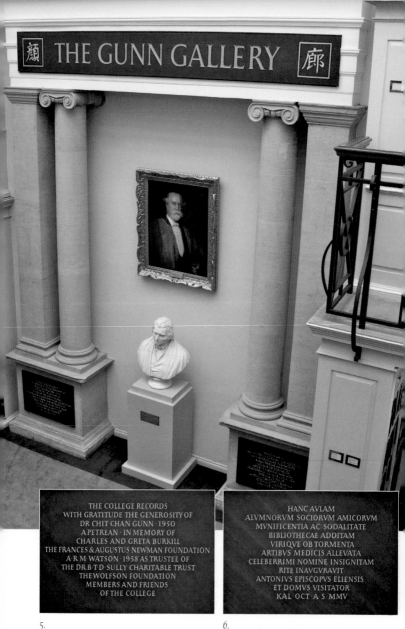

THE GUNN GALLERY

THE COLLEGE RECORDS
WITH GRATITUDE THE GENEROSITY OF
DR CHIT CHAN GUNN · 1950
A PETREAN · IN MEMORY OF
CHARLES AND GRETA BURKILL
THE FRANCES & AUGUSTUS NEWMAN FOUNDATION
A·R·M·WATSON · 1958 AS TRUSTEE OF
THE DR B·T·D·SULLY CHARITABLE TRUST
THE WOLFSON FOUNDATION
MEMBERS AND FRIENDS
OF THE COLLEGE

HANC AVLAM
ALVMNORVM SOCIORVM AMICORVM
MVNIFICENTIA AC SODALITATE
BIBLIOTHECAE ADDITAM
VIRIQVE OB TORMENTA
ARTIBVS MEDICIS ALLEVATA
CELEBERRIMI NOMINE INSIGNITAM
RITE INAVGVRAVIT
ANTONIVS EPISCOPVS ELIENSIS
ET DOMVS VISITATOR
KAL·OCT·A·S·MMV

5.   6.

2005 slate across them, naming *The Gunn Gallery*, including
the Chinese characters for Dr Chan Gunn.[4] The plinths bear two
further gilded benefactors' slates.[5 & 6]

There are many brass plates in this Library. They
commemorate past pupils, fellows and benefactors. The '*D.D.*'
appearing on them is for *DONO DEDIT*, 'given as a gift'.
The plates are to be found on bookcases, table
tops, chair backs, or sculpture plinths.[7]

The College Hall has a 2008 brass plate
on the wall between the two doors, for
Richard Wilson Harris and his widow.[8]

7. All the library's brasses
are in Lida's own typeface:
Emilida. This is unique to
the Workshop.

MRS EPSTEIN IN A MANTILLA 1918 · JACOB EPSTEIN
BEQUEATHED TO THE COLLEGE BY EDWARD SHILS 1910-1995· FELLOW AND HONORARY FELLOW

3.

To
mark
the first visit of
HER MAJESTY
THE QUEEN
Patroness
8th June
2005

Note the contrast
between the
lettering (e.g. all
capitals) for a
solemn 50 years
occasion, and the
more jaunty italic
setting for a new
patron's debut at
the college.

TO COMMEMORATE THE VISIT OF
HER MAJESTY QUEEN ELIZABETH THE QUEEN MOTHER
ON 9TH JUNE 1998, MARKING THE 50TH ANNIVERSARY OF
HER MAJESTY'S FIRST VISIT AS PATRONESS

2.

Queens' College

*Margaret of Anjou (Queen to Henry VI) and Elizabeth Woodville
(Queen to Edward IV) are the two foundresses between 1448
and 1465. So the apostrophe ought to be at the end, but this is
19th century pedantry. Erasmus, a distinguished early resident,
always called it Collegium Reginae.*

*A 1961 Swedish Green marble stone for the opening of
the Erasmus Building (outside south wall) marks the long
association of Queen Elizabeth (Queen Mother) as patroness.[1]
The 50th anniversary of her first visit is celebrated by a 1998
green slate[2]; it is in the old college entrance passage near Queens'
Lane. Alongside is another green slate, for the first visit in 2005
of the new patroness, Queen Elizabeth.[3]*

West of the river the
Cripps Building has
three 2007 engraved
glass pieces on the
4th floor of the north
wing. A glass panel
with blue lettering by
Seminar Room 2
records thanks to 12 donors
'who enabled the college
to construct this building'.[4]

On the same corridor, two etched windows facing south name the
Stephen Thomas Teaching & Research Centre[5], with a quotation
from him:

> Life is a succession of moments
> To live each one is to succeed.

The college's sports grounds are out on the Barton Road beyond
the city boundary; on a wall inside a pavilion here there is a
lime wood tablet (1965)[6]: THE VENN PAVILION erected in
honour of John Archibald Venn.

Robinson College

David Robinson worked in his father's bicycle shop as a lad;
Sir David died in 1987 as the remarkable philanthropist who
had made his fortune in the TV rental business. He founded his
college (1980) in record time: building took just 3 years.

The chapel's handsome 2001 Massangis (French limestone)
inscription is on the wall of the steps going up to the gallery at
the south end, and marks Lord Lewis' long-held project for this
link.[1] It too was done in record time, after heart-stopping delays
in getting the stone from France.

1. Italic letters throughout – they were carefully painted in a dark red colour.

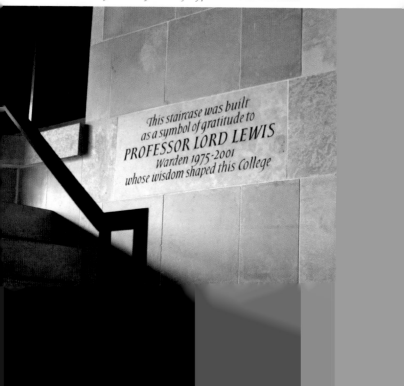

St Catharine's College

The college begun by Robert Woodlark in 1473 with a Master and 3 Fellows was rebuilt in the 17th century, and saw further major changes in the 20th.

Its coat of arms was carved in Ketton stone in 1952, and can be seen above the entrance to the Porters' Lodge in the Woodlark Building.[1] There is an inscribed silver plate at the base of a decorated wooden bowl from 1955 (not on view), commissioned by the Senior Tutor – a first attempt at this in other hands had 'gone wrong and must be redesigned'.[2]

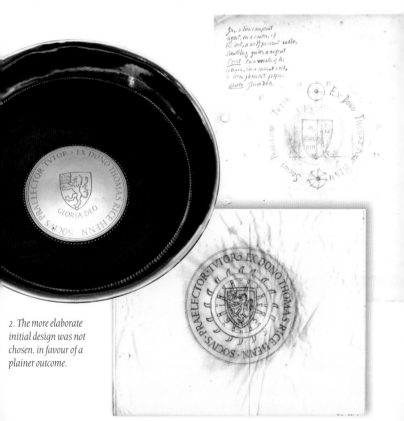

2. The more elaborate
initial design was not
chosen, in favour of a
plainer outcome.

St Edmund's College

This graduate college, founded in 1896, has seen considerable expansion in recent decades. So the Duke of Edinburgh's visit in 1987 was an occasion for a Welsh slate by the entrance to the Dining Hall (bear right after going into the entrance lobby). It has the Duke's heraldic badge on top.[1] Another Welsh slate is inside an entrance to the Richard Laws Building for its 2002 opening, again by the Duke.[2]

This plaque was unveiled by HIS ROYAL HIGHNESS THE DUKE OF EDINBURGH CHANCELLOR of THE UNIVERSITY of CAMBRIDGE who visited the College on Friday 12th June 1987

The pillars either side of the entrance drive said 'Saint Edmunds Hall' until 1987; the Workshop was then given the tricky task of changing 'Hall' to 'College'.[3]

St John's College

*The Foundress, Lady Margaret Beaufort, King Henry VII's
mother, had already 'done' Christ's College; it is said that
when it came to St John's in 1511, the endowment had
to be largely land alas, rather than riches. Alas indeed:
St John's soon became foremost in Cambridge (with Trinity)
for size and possessions.*

*Just as progressing through the St John's courts is reported
to be a journey through English
architectural history, its ante-
chapel gives a 60 year view
of the Workshop story.*

1.

1. *The most recent addition to the ante-chapel wall, from design to carving: creative energy has to be carried forward from the idea into the chisel, without faltering for even a moment.*

There are 14 stones for past Fellows from 1953 to 2010. And there is social history in the linking records: commissioning letters from the early years addressed brusquely 'Dear Kindersley', with replies about now unbelievable costs at under £50 a stone. In deciding on the material for the 1978 piece, David Kindersley wrote 'we try and ring the changes as regards the stone, so as to make the wall just that bit more interesting than it would otherwise be'. So we have[1]:

3 Nabresina marble	*(Sikes 1960; Palmer* & White* 1970)*
2 Portland stone	*(Howard 1959; Ratcliff* 1969)*
2 Solstone	*(Bartlett 1971; Constable 1978)*
2 Welsh slate	*(Benians* 1955 with Portland stone moulding;Fleming 1956)*
Yellow Mansfield stone	*(Charlesworth* 1953)*
Hopton Wood stone	*(Raven* 1953, with a 1992 addition for his wife Esther Margaret)*
Caen stone	*(Rootham* 1953)*
Comblanchien – a French Limestone	*(Howland* 1997, with a 2001 addition for his wife Eileen)*
Ancaster stone	*(Boys Smith and his wife* 2010)*

* illustrated

6. *The glass was engraved in situ, using a dentist's drill – another delight of working in Cambridge.*

JEAN
CURTIS
1942-1989
Assistant
Librarian

3. This four-and-a-half metre long seat was cut in situ into stones of different hardness and colour. We rested on our knees, contrary to usual Workshop practice. The upright position has three important advantages: we can judge proportions/lay-out and step back for a better view; we stand or sit upright with a straight back rather than crouch; the dust from the cut falls away with no need for brushing, which would also erase our pencilled setting-out.

4. *Glass panels were sandblasted in rustic Roman capital letters, and then placed up in their ceiling positions.*

The ante-chapel's War Memorial had 3 names added in 1972, and another in 1996.[2]

In the Library there are half a dozen more recent pieces. Downstairs a stone bench has a much elongated inscription remembering Ernest Frank Bill Williams (1995).[3] Upstairs 'The John Hall Law Library' is on two glass panels from the ceiling, etched/sand blasted (1994).[4] En route to the older Upper Library a bookcase on the left carries a small 1995 brass plate for Norman Charles Buck.[5] Once upstairs, look for an engaging engraving-in-situ of a glass window pane in the west wall: Jean Curtis, Assistant Librarian (1990).[6]

Selwyn College

George Augustus Selwyn was the first Bishop of New Zealand (1841–68), then at Lichfield (1868–78). The college founded in his name commissioned a sundial in 2009 [1]; 'On the making of a sundial', on page 12, illustrates how it was made.

London's 17th century (and pre-Great Fire church) St Katharine Cree in Leadenhall Street is the only other place in the country to have such a sundial, including Babylonian and Italian hours. The Selwyn sundial does not have the expected rod (gnomon) for throwing a shadow. Instead there is a short stub with a disc (nodus): the shadow indicating time is a round blob. This documents hours since sunrise (gilded lines) or since sunset (white lines). Babylon (left) and Italy (right) are explained in lettering on the bottom edge.

The Latin inscription is for the benefactor: 'a Yorkshire dairyman gave me to his college for a gift'. The Greek is 'Know the time', with the subtext 'seize your opportunity'.

1.

Sidney Sussex College

Lady Frances Sidney was a great figure at Queen Elizabeth's court; the wordly woman came to leave a will that led to the foundation of her college in 1596. The site had been occupied by the Grey Friars (Franciscans) for 300 years before.

The ante-chapel has a Welsh slate on the right from 1978 for a past Master, John Wilfrid Linnett [1]; with a 2005 addition 'and of his wife Rae Ellen'. [2] In the Chapel itself, on the east wall, an oak panel is inscribed for Thomas Henry Lyon, architect (1986). [3] David Kindersley wanted to carve this on one of the horizontal panels, the college preferred a vertical one, and he commented 'I think a good job on a rather nasty bit of oak'.

Outside in South Court, on an east wall, there is a 1990 Welsh slate for Dr Smail – note how the affectionate 'Otto' has been set off against his more formal names. [4]

In memory of
JOHN WILFRID
LINNETT
3 August 1913 - 7 November 1975
FELLOW OF
THE ROYAL SOCIETY
PROFESSOR OF
PHYSICAL CHEMISTRY
MASTER
OF THIS COLLEGE
1970 - 1975
VICE - CHANCELLOR
1973 - 1975
and of his wife
RAE ELLEN
30 August 1918 - 24 March 2005

1 & 2. A 27 year span separates the first cutting of this stone, and its second inscription for the widow. This was all planned from the start, and completed by thinking along similar lines; i.e. not slavishly copying the original.

4.

The 1991 bridge across Sussex Street is marked by two keystones
east and west outside; one with the college arms[5], the other with
the Sidney heraldic beast, a porcupine.[6] They are carved and
painted, using platinum rather than silver leaf (which would
turn black). The unusual Guiting stone here comes
from Gloucestershire.

Inside the bridge
walkway, low on the west
wall, is a small marble
tablet for designer and
architect, also 1991.[7]

THIS BRIDGE
WAS DESIGNED BY
PETER SALT
FELLOW OF THE COLLEGE &
FRANCIS HOOKHAM
ARCHITECT
1990

7.

5.

6.

David Kindersley is sealing the stone using white oil-based paint; then it is varnished with goldsize before applying platinum leaf for the porcupine's spines.

Trinity College

Henry VIII's foundation dates from 1546, combining
Michaelhouse and King's Hall which had been on the Cambridge
scene for two centuries before. The roll call of the college's great and
famous, from Isaac Newton on, is astounding.

Everything at Trinity is on a large scale – and that includes
the Workshop's contributions. They begin in 1951 in the ante-
chapel, where the interior had to be reorganized in order to fit the

massive Portland stone for the 1939–45 War Memorial on the west wall.[1] Here 382 names (some 4050 letters) were inscribed. Inevitably omissions came to light, as well as (delightfully unexpected) survivors: in 1958/9 four alterations were made to this roll of honour.

1. Following Prof. Sir Albert Richardson's basic plan, David Kindersley was chosen for this massive commission, designing and cutting everything in situ. The letters in the top and bottom lines are gilded, deep cut (9 mm), and huge (23 cm high on top). The individual names are tinted red.

The ante-chapel has its panelled walls lined with the 'Trinity Brasses': tablets commemorating former distinguished Fellows.[2] The Workshop's 82 plates make a 50 year sequence, from Ralph Howard Fowler (1952) to Robert Robson (2006). En route there are many luminaries; illustrated are Ralph Vaughan Williams (1962) and Bertrand Russell (1970).

Off the ante-chapel, on a wall of the eastern room of the Choir Vestry, there is a handsome oval Welsh slate for Basil Denis Dennis-Jones (1969).[3] In the Chapel itself the altar has a long 1952 Latin inscription beginning AD MAJOREM DEI[4]; it runs just below the altar top, carved directly into the wood.

2. Two of the 82 brasses done by the workshop here. One is all in capitals, the other also uses lower case letters; every plate is an individual design.

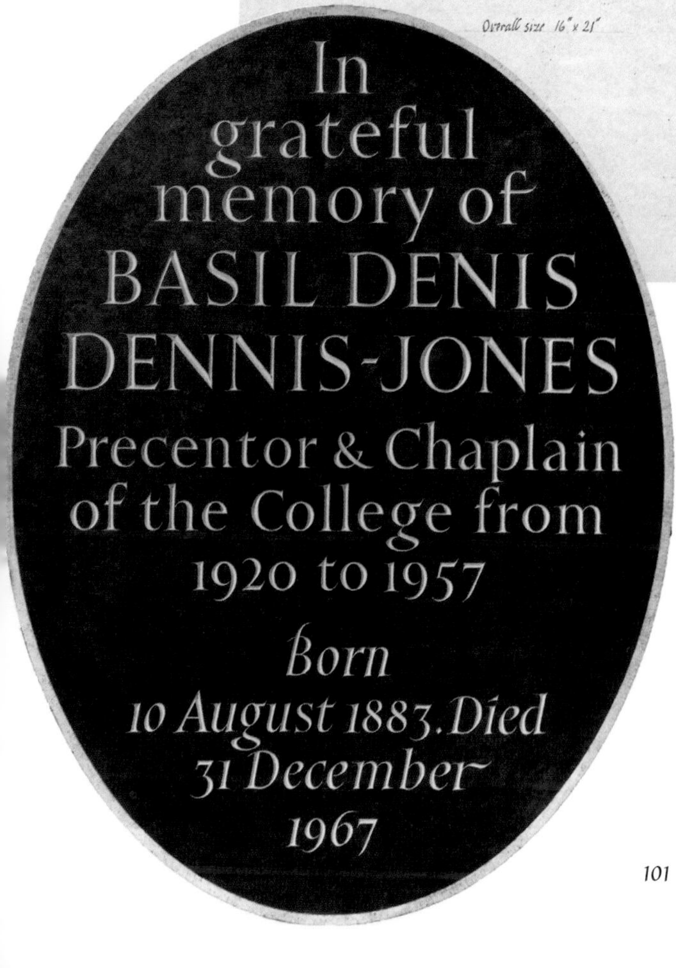

3. *From scale design to final plaque: the Workshop has a comprehensive archive going back to 1930, keeping correspondence, designs and rubbings as a permanent record.*

Shallow chiselled rebate

In
grateful
memory of
BASIL DENIS
DENNIS-JONES
Precentor & Chaplain
of the College from
1920 to 1957

Born
10 August 1883. Died
31 December
1967

Overall size 16" x 21"

David Kindersley's
Chesterton Tower, Chesterton
Cambridge. Drawn by
August 1968.

In
grateful
memory of
BASIL DENIS
DENNIS-JONES
Precentor & Chaplain
of the College from
1920 to 1957

Born
10 August 1883. Died
31 December
1967

In the college buildings east across Trinity Street, bear right into the entrance hall of the Wolfson Building, for a 1973 yellow inscription to the benefactors[5]; it runs along the brick wall. And west across Queen's Road there is the new development of Burrell's Field, opened by the Queen in 1996. A Welsh slate by the pond marks the occasion.[6]

A weather-beaten Welsh slate of 1963 is right on a roof parapet of Angel Court; architects, builders and bursars are commemorated here, but access is only for the hardy (frontispiece).[7]

This room
is named in memory
of
SIR HERSCH
LAUTERPACHT QC·LLD
Born 1897 ~ Died 1960
Whewell Professor of
International Law in
this University 1937·54
Judge of the
International Court
of Justice
1954·60

Masoning an oval is slow business – like everything when working in stone : the bevel or moulding makes an elegant complement to the whole piece.

Trinity Hall

Founded by Bishop Bateman in 1350, who stipulated 'promotion of divine worship and of canon and civil science' – the Black Death had also decimated clergymen and lawyers. Law studies remain a strong tradition.

The chapel contains a 1952 Memorial Book of the Fallen, calligraphed by the Workshop, but not on view.[1] 1998 saw the building of the Jerwood Library, marked by 3 stones. A Welsh slate naming it is on the outside west wall above the river.[2] The name is also carved into the stonework for the 'Q' archway inside the college[3], near another Welsh slate for the opening of the Library (1999).[4] This reads:

2. We had to arrange scaffolding in the water for fixing this slate.

'This Library was opened on 15 May 1999 by THE RIGHT HONOURABLE THE LORD HOWE OF ABERAVON CH QC on the occasion of the Annual Gathering of the Trinity Hall Association in the presence of ALAN GRIEVE Chairman of the Jerwood Foundation'.

The college has further buildings on the Wychfield site in Storey's Way. The 2006 Foundation Stone here, in Portland stone, revives the series of Trinity Hall milestones that grace the route from Great St Mary's Church to Barkway in Hertfordshire.[5] The milestone is in the hedge on the eastern side of Storey's Way, and combines old and new: there is the traditional college motif, but the distances are in metres, and direct to the Wychfield and main college sites.

5. The surface of the Portland stone was cut back, leaving the hands and heraldry raised. We followed the tradition of reversing black/white for the college arms, for instant recognition along the road.

Wolfson College

Founded by the University in 1965
as the graduate University College,
a generous benefaction made it
Wolfson College in 1973; the residents
include mature undergraduates.

A tall standing stone of
asymmetric shape and lettering for
the college's name (Elterwater Green
slate 2010) marks its rear entrance
in Selwyn Gardens.[1]

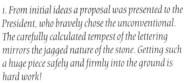

1. From initial ideas a proposal was presented to the
President, who bravely chose the unconventional.
The carefully calculated tempest of the lettering
mirrors the jagged nature of the stone. Getting such
a huge piece safely and firmly into the ground is
hard work!

Part II · Catalogue of works

Catalogue

Christ's College

1.	1989	Dr Szeming SZE	Brass	10 × 38
2.	1990	Monica Mary KORNBERG	Bronze	6 × 14
3.	1995	Edward Kenny LEVICK	Wood in situ (alteration)	
	1998	Douglas ROBSON	Wood in situ (addition)	

Churchill College

1.	2002	Winston CHURCHILL	'Portland stone'	80 × 1350
2.	1989	Jock COLVILLE	Welsh slate	118 × 70
3.	2002	Various sand-blasted panels including major benefactors	Glass	125 × 50
4.	1991	MAERSK MC-KINNEY (Foundation)	Portland stone	74 × 145
5.	1992	QUEEN INGRID (Opening)	Portland stone	30 × 78

Clare College

1.	1950	War Memorial case	Walnut & Hopton Wood stone corbels	101 × 81

2.	2006	Christopher RUTTER	Brass	5 × 16
3.	2000	Paul MELLON	Ketton stone in situ	63
4.	2008	Sir David ATTENBOROUGH	Brass	6 × 22

Clare Hall

1.	1997	Brian PIPPARD	Welsh slate	51 × 86
2.	1999	Leslie BARNETT	Welsh slate	51 × 36
3.	2000	Gillian BEER	Welsh slate	79 × 66
4.	2000	Paul MELLON	Welsh slate	53 × 97
5.	2000	Robert HONEYCOMBE	Welsh slate	36 × 102
6.	2000	Michael STOKER	Welsh slate	61 × 76
7.	2000	Anthony LOW	Welsh slate	88 × 29
8.	1997	Libby GARDNER	Welsh slate (×4)	20 × 201
			+ 4 pieces	20 × 20
9.	2008	Sanae ASAHARA	Welsh slate	100 × 26
10.	1997	John Arthur GARROD	Portland stone (4 pieces)	201 × 20

Corpus Christi College

1.	1978	Sir George THOMSON	Brass	18 × 25
2.	2008	TAYLOR LIBRARY	stone in situ	220
3.	2008	T, X, Y & disabled sign	stone in situ	20 × 20
4.	2007	Library Window	4 glass panels	73 × 258
				64 × 258
				60 × 258
				180 × 85
5.	2008	Corpus Clock	Bath stone	85 × 135
6.	2007	INSALL & FREEMAN	Ancaster stone	63 × 122

7.	2008	GIRDLERS' ROOM	Welsh slate	16 × 82
8.	2008	Library bookshelves	Wood blocks (27 capital letters, 12 tablets)	
9.	2007	Librarian's stationery	Letterheads	
10.	1950	Pelican Column (Grantchester)	Portland stone	height 300
11.	2006	Michael McCRUM (Grantchester)	Green slate	122 × 46

Darwin College

1.	1969	Foundation	Portland stone	99 × 160

Downing College

1.	2007	Stephen FLEET	Welsh slate	40 × 45

Emmanuel College

1.	1993	Queen's Building (Foundation)	Ketton stone	57 × 69
2/3.	1995	Queen's Building (Opening)	Italian slate (×2)	600 × 1600
4/5.	1995	LAING & FRANCK Rooms	Polished plaster in situ	135
6.	2002	WORLD WAR II	Welsh slate	36 × 41

Fitzwilliam College

1.	1993	F. Peter WILSON (Foundation)	Portland stone	44 × 66
2.	1995	FIRST UNDERGRADUATE	Welsh slate	47 × 30

Girton College

1.	1952–1976	Girton Chapel		
		Individual Oak Panels in situ		26 × 59

1953	MARGARET SWAINSON ANDERSON
1966	JANET RUTH BACON
1966	MARIE ADRIENNE HENRIETTE BIBAS
1968	HELEN MAUD CAM
1965	MARY CLOVER
1976	ETHEL SOPHIA FEGAN
1978	MARJORIE TAPPAN HOLLOND
1952	NORAE CHRISTINAE JOLLIFFE
1956	MARY GWLADYS JONES
1958	PAULINE KATHERINE LEVESON
1955	HILDA L. LORIMER
1952	HILDA MARY RUTHVEN MURRAY
1974	KATHLEEN MARY PEACE
1969	KATHLEEN MARJORIE ROBERTSON
1955	MARY BEATRICE THOMAS
1969	HILDA JOAN VLASTO

Composite Boards

1952	MARGARET ALFORD
1971	DAME MADELINE DOROTHY BROCK
1958	EDITH MARY BROWN
1966	MARY AUGUSTA VERE COCHRAN
1971	SYBIL CREED
1971	CYNTHIA MARY CREWS
1966	HENRIETTE DENT
1966	ELIZABETH DREW
1955	DOROTHY EVERETT
1966	MARY FLETCHER
1974	MARY DOROTHY GEORGE

	1961	ALICE ADéLE GUY		
	1968	FLORENCE ELIZABETH HARMER		
	1961	CHARLOTTE ANNA PAULINE LEUBUSCHER		
	1974	ELEANOR LADY NATHAN OF CHURT		
	1961	ETHELWYN RAMSAY PEARSON		
	1974	GISELA MARIA AUGUSTA RICHTER		
	1958	HILDA VISCOUNTESS RUNCIMAN		
	1952	CAROLINE ANNE JAMES SKEEL		
	1971	MARGARET SMITH		
	1954	MARY SYBIL SMITH		
	1974	DOROTHY TARRANT		
	1958	SOPHIE TRENKNER		
	1958	DOROTHY JOAN WILSON		
	1971	WINIFRED FERGUSON YOUNG		
2.	1952	Kathleen Teresa Blake BUTLER	Welsh slate with Caen stone mouldings	60 × 70
3.	1952	Katharine JEX-BLAKE	Portland stone with marble capping	57 × 72
4.	1952	Edith Helen MAJOR	Portland stone with Black Hopton Wood capping	56 × 41
5.	1965	Helen Marion WODEHOUSE	Nabresina marble	56 × 75
6.	2003	Mary CARTWRIGHT	Jerusalem Gold	70 × 94
7.	1969	Thomas McMORRAN	Darley Dale stone	85 × 61
8.	1969	Helen Isabelle McMORRAN	Oak	58 × 41
9.	1956	CHEMICAL LABORATORY	Paint & plywood	25 × 25

Gonville & Caius College (West Road)

1.	2005	Neil McKENDRICK (Foundation)	Ancaster Hard White	100 × 100
2.	2008	Stephen Hawking Building (Opening)	stone in situ	10 × 580
3.	2008	Stephen Hawking Building (DONALD INSALL)	stone in situ	4 × 102

Homerton College

1.	1957	Coat of Arms	Ketton stone	98 × 91
2.	1957	QUEEN ELIZABETH (Opening)	Ketton stone in situ	78
3.	1973	HOMERTON COLLEGE	Portland stone (×2)	69 × 136

Hughes Hall

1.	2005	Opening	Welsh slate	16 × 189

Jesus College

1.	1973	FREDERICI BRITTAIN	Oak doors in situ (×2)	116 × 42
2.	1972	14 Corbels in the Hall	Repainting & regilding	
3.	1961	GULIELMI WELSH	Nabresina marble	65 × 140
4.	1967	MORTAL MAN	Westmorland green slate	12 × 22
5.	1969	FB	Ketton stone in situ	10 × 15

King's College

1.	1950	Herbert William RICHMOND	Welsh slate	41 × 46
		Additional:		
	1958	The College could not trace an inscription for a lost Stephen Glanville memorial.		

Lucy Cavendish College

1.	1993	Dame Anne WARBURTON	Portland stone	44 × 66

Magdalene College

1.	1967	Nigel THOMSON	stone in situ	8 × 118
2.	2002	Robert LATHAM	Brass	18 × 12
3.	2004	Michael RAMSEY	Brass	24 × 10
4.	2006	A. S. RAMSEY	Brass	6 × 14
5.	2006	PRAESIDES	Brass	30 × 14
6.	2001	GOETZE & GWYNN ORGAN	Brass	40 × 16
7.	2005	CRIPPS COURT	stone in situ	20 × 180
8.	2005	GARDE TA FOY	stone in situ	45 × 180
9.	2005	EDWARD & ROBERT CRIPPS	Welsh slate	46 × 91
10.	2005	CRIPPS COURT (Opening)	Welsh slate	46 × 91

Murray Edwards College (New Hall)

1.	1957	Eliza WILKINSON	Brass	9 × 18

Newnham College

1.	1965	Edith Marjorie MARTLAND	Welsh slate	20 × 25

Pembroke College

1.	1950	Coat of arms	Clipsham stone	107 × 102
2.	1956	SISTE TE PAULUM	Slate (recut & coloured)	78 × 87
3.	1971	Two bookplates for Sydney Castle & Marjorie ROBERTS		5 ×8
4.		Silverware		

	1977	Wood inscription on base of silver dish, presented by the College to Stanley Chown.		
	1978	Two sauce boats engraved D. D. Bryan Earle King, with the College coat of arms.		
	1980	Two sauce boats engraved 'memor esto dilecti amici B. W. quondam praesidis', also with coat of arms.		
	1981	Engraved quaich 'given by Colin Gilbraith for the Burns Dinner 1981'.		
5.	1998	Sundial	stone cut in situ	Height 260
		Additional:		
	1988	A brass plate naming the former Master's Lodge is no longer traceable.		

Peterhouse

1.	1957	RICARDI HENRICI LOVELOCK LEE	Ketton stone in situ	170
2.	1998	DG	York stone	30 × 45
3.	1984	HANC BIBLIOTHECAM	Cumbrian Green slate	51 × 110
4.	2005	GUNN GALLERY	Slate	38 × 336
5.	2005	THE COLLEGE RECORDS WITH	Slate	51 × 75
6.	2005	HANC AVLAM ALVMNORVM	Slate	51 × 75
7.		Library Brasses		
	1984	Bookcases		
		T. G. ASKWITH & T. M. N. ASKWITH		
		A. C. C. BAXTER		
		H. BEACH		
		I. CURTIS, J. S. CURTIS & F. J. CURTIS		

L. A. G. DRESEL

J. R. HALL

E. J. KENNEY

STANDARD TELEPHONES AND CABLES plc

Tables

E. T. GOODWIN

F. C. HAPPOLD, E. C. HAPPOLD
& D. C. D. HAPPOLD

A. G. JOHNSTONE, M. A. JOHNSTONE
& H. S. G. JOHNSTONE

C. S. MARRIOTT & D. G. MARRIOTT

1985   *Sculpture plinth on mezzanine floor*

PAST, PRESENT, FUTURE BY JACK HAZZARD

2005   *Bookcases*

THE FRIENDS OF PETERHOUSE

THE LATE H. B. GOTTSCHALK

M. E. C. MORE O'FERRALL

A. J. WILLIAMS

Chair backs

1985   PEHIN DATO, B. H. KHOO, K. J. TAN & H. G. ANG

2005   THE HARDINGHAM TRUST

P. J. HAWKES

A. J. MCINTYRE

A. P. POWER

D. M. TURNER

2008   DATO LAU FOO SUN

TO'PUAN LAU-GUNN CHIT WHA IN HONOREM
TIFFANY TIAN LI LAU

TO'PUAN LAU-GUNN CHIT WHA IN HONOREM
BRANDON TIAN WEI LAU

	2005	Tables		
		C. J. CARTER		
		A. S. CLARK		
		THE LATE L. A. G. DRESEL		
		Busts		
	1989	JOHN GRAHAME DOUGLAS CLARKE		
	2005	MRS EPSTEIN IN A MANTILLA. JACOB EPSTEIN		
	2006	Tabletop Gunn Gallery		
		IN MEMORIAM F. J. SHAW		
8.	2008	Richard WILSON HARRIS	Brass	16 × 13

Queens' College

1.	1961	QUEEN ELIZABETH (Erasmus Opening)	Swedish Green marble	76 × 137
2.	1998	QUEEN ELIZABETH THE QUEEN MOTHER	Green slate	36 × 107
3.	2005	HER MAJESTY THE QUEEN	Green slate	81 × 61
4.	2007	QUEENS' COLLEGE CAMBRIDGE THANKS THE DONORS	Glass panel	35 × 140
5.	2007	Stephen THOMAS Teaching Centre	Glass windows (×2)	240 × 108
6.	1965	John Archibald VENN	Lime wood	24 × 57

Robinson College

1.	2001	Lord LEWIS	Massangis stone	37 × 92

St Catharine's College

1.	1952	Coat of Arms	Ketton stone	85 × 120
2.	1955	Thomas Rice HENN	Wooden Bowl Plate	12 × 12

St Edmund's College

1.	1987	HIS ROYAL HIGHNESS	Welsh slate	66 × 66
2.	2002	Richard LAWS (Opening)	Welsh slate	61 × 76
3.	1987	St Edmund's College	Alteration from 'Hall'. Stone in situ (×2)	6 × 40

St John's College

1.	1953–2001	St John's Ante-Chapel Stones		
	1971	FREDERICK CHARLES BARTLETT	Solstone	19 × 38
	1955	ERNEST ALFRED BENIANS	Welsh slate with Portland stone moulding	40 × 58
	2010	JOHN SANDWITH BOYS SMITH	Ancaster stone	20 × 38
	1953	MARTIN PERCIVAL CHARLESWORTH	Yellow Mansfield stone	19 × 38
	1978	WILLIAM GEORGE CONSTABLE	Solstone	19 × 40
	1956	JOHN AMBROSE FLEMING	Welsh slate	27 × 51
	1959	HENRY FRASER HOWARD	Portland stone	19 × 41
	1997	ROBERT LESLIE HOWLAND	Comblanchien	20 × 38
	2001	and his wife EILEEN	"	"
	1970	WILLIAM GEORGE PALMER	Nabresina marble	18 × 38
	1969	EDWARD CRADDOCK RATCLIFF	Portland stone	18 × 38
	1953	EDWARD EARLE RAVEN	Hopton Wood stone	19 × 38
	1992	(+) ESTHER MARGARET	"	"
	1953	CYRIL BRADLEY ROOTHAM	Caen stone	19 × 38

	1960	EDWARD ERNEST SIKES	Nabresina marble	17 × 40
	1970	FRANCIS PURYER WHITE	Nabresina marble	19 × 38
2.		Ante-Chapel War Memorial additions		
	1972	N. G. DAVIES	Marble	
	1972	T. E. HULME	Marble	
	1972	G. H. MAY	Marble	
	1996	J. H. WAINWRIGHT	Marble	
3.	1995	Ernest Frank Bill WILLIAMS	Stone Bench	74× 455
4.	1994	JOHN HALL LIBRARY	Glass panels (×2)	79 × 137
5.	1995	Norman Charles BUCK	Brass	14 × 14
6.	1990	Jean CURTIS	Window glass in situ	14 × 11

Selwyn College

1.	2010	Sundial	Welsh slate	86 × 107

Sidney Sussex College

1.	1978	John Wilfrid LINNETT	Welsh slate	71 × 61
2.	2005	and of his wife RAE ELLEN	"	"
3.	1986	Thomas Henry LYON	Oak panel in situ	188 × 72
4.	1990	Raymond Charles Otto SMAIL	Welsh slate	77 × 52
5.	1991	Keystone – Coat of Arms	Guiting stone	90 × 45
6.	1991	Keystone – Porcupine	Guiting stone	90 × 45
7.	1991	SALT & HOOKHAM	Marble	27 × 46

Trinity College

1.	1951	PRO MURO ERANT NOBIS	Portland stone in situ	Length 950
			(War Memorial)	

2.	Trinity Ante-Chapel Brasses (of the order of 20 × 45)	
1987	HERBERT MAYOW ADAMS	
1991	JOHN FRANK ADAMS	
1963	GVILELMI IOSCELYN ARKELL	
1953	FRANCIS WILLIAM ASTON	
1974	ABRAHAM SAMOILOVITCH BESICOVITCH	
1988	ALFRED MAURICE BINNIE	
1976	MAURICE BLACK	
1973	WILLIAM LAWRENCE BRAGG	
1972	CHARLIE DUNBAR BROAD	
1970	BENJAMIN CHAPMAN BROWNE	
1953	FRANCIS CRAWFORD BURKITT	
1980	JOHN BURNABY	
1977	JAMES RAMSAY MONTAGU BUTLER	
1984	RICHARD AUSTEN BUTLER BARO de SAFFRON WALDEN	
1953	JOHN WALTON CAPSTICK	
1986	EDWARD HALLETT CARR	
1953	FRANCIS MACDONALD CORNFORD	
1969	HENRICUS HALLETT DALE	
1955	WILLIAM CECIL DAMPIER	
1971	HAROLD DAVENPORT	
1966	DISCIPULUS SOCIUS	(28 × 8)
1980	MAURICE HERBERT DOBB	
1993	PATRICK WILLIAM DUFF	
1958	FREDERICUS JACOBUS DYKES	
1954	SIR ARTHUR STANLEY EDDINGTON	

1966	HENRICI OVTRAM EVENETT
1952	RALPH HOWARD FOWLER
1954	JACOBUS GEORGIUS FRAZER
1982	OTTO ROBERT FRISCH
1986	JOHN ANDREW GALLAGHER
1969	GEORGE PEABODY GOOCH
1979	ANDREW SYDENHAM FARRAR GOW
1991	CHARLES JOHN HAMSON
1954	GODFREY HAROLD HARDY
1954	ERNEST HARRISON
1955	ARTHUR GILBERT HINKS
2001	ALAN LLOYD HODGKIN
1976	HENRY ARTHUR HOLLOND
1955	SIR FREDERICK EDWARD HOPKINS
1953	HUGH MCLEOD INNES
1987	PIOTR LEOMDOVITCH KAPITZA
1968	ALANUS KER
1977	GEORGE SIDNEY ROBERTS KITSON CLARK
1965	ARTHUR HAROLD JOHN KNIGHT
1953	GAILLARD THOMAS LAPSLEY
1989	RALPH ALEXANDER LEIGH
1963	GERALDI PONSONBY LENOX-CONYNGHAM
1979	JOHN EDERSON LITTLEWOOD
1986	FREDERICK GEORGE MANN
1962	HUBERT STANLEY MIDDLETON
1962	GEORGE EDWARD MOORE (1991 date correction)
1953	HUGH FRANK NEWALL
1992	TRESSILIAN CHARLES NICHOLAS

1962   REYNOLD ALLEYNE NICHOLSON

1967   CARL FREDERICK ABEL PANTIN

1954   DAVID ALFRED CHILTON PEARSON

1971   MARK GILLACHRIST MARLBOROUGH PRYOR

1991   SRINIVASA RAMANUJAN

1971   ROBERT MANTLE RATTENBURY

1965   DENIS HOLME ROBERTSON

1962   DONALD STRUAN ROBERTSON

1987   JOHN ARTHUR THOMAS ROBINSON

2006   ROBERT ROBSON

1974   FRANCIS JOHN WORSLEY ROUGHTON

1986   WILLIAM ALBERT HUGH RUSHTON

1970   BERTRAND RUSSELL

1988   MARTIN RYLE

1993   FRANCIS HENRY SANDBACH

1974   FREDERICK ARTHUR SIMPSON

1987   PIERO SRAFFA

1953   HUGO FRASER STEWART

1978   GEOFFREY INGRAM TAYLOR

1958   FREDERICUS ROBERTUS TENNANT

1953   GEORGE MACAULAY TREVELYAN

1991   WALTER ULLMANN

1962   RALPH VAUGHAN WILLIAMS

2001   JOHN MICHAEL KENNETH VYVYAN

1956   ALFRED NORTH WHITEHEAD

1952   DENYS ARTHUR WINSTANLEY

1968   CARL WINTER

1996   ARTHUR JOHN TERENCE DIBBEN WISDOM

	1963	LVDOVICVS WITTGENSTEIN		
3.	1969	Basil Dennis DENNIS-JONES	Welsh slate	53 × 41
4.	1952	AD MAJOREM DEI	Altar wood in situ	Length 270
5a.	1973	WOLFSON BUILDING	Brick wall in situ	Length 268
5b.	1973	BUILT 1969–71	Brick wall in situ	Length 860
6.	1996	BURRELL'S FIELD (Opening)	Welsh slate	38 × 91
7.	1963	ANGEL COURT	Welsh slate	50 × 113
		Additional:		
	1965	Oval Portland stone naming a room for Sir Hersch LAUTERPACHT	now at 5 Cranmer Road (Lauterpacht International Law Centre)	77 × 61
	1972	Brass plate for Lady Carr, a benefactor of a suite of refurbished rooms	now Junior Parlour	
	1995	2 brass plates, for Malaysian Commonwealth Studies Centre & Pok Raffeah House	now on outside wall at 11 Madingley Road	

Trinity Hall

1.	1952	Chapel Memorial Book '1939 – 1945'	Names inscribed	
2.	1999	THE JERWOOD LIBRARY 1998	Welsh slate	61 × 61
3.	1999	JERWOOD LIBRARY	Stone in situ	30 × 53
4.	1999	THE LORD HOWE (Opening)	Welsh slate	69 × 99
5.	2006	Milestone AD MMVI (Foundation)	Portland stone	110 × 40

Wolfson College

1.	2010	Wolfson College	Elterwater Green slate	160 × 70

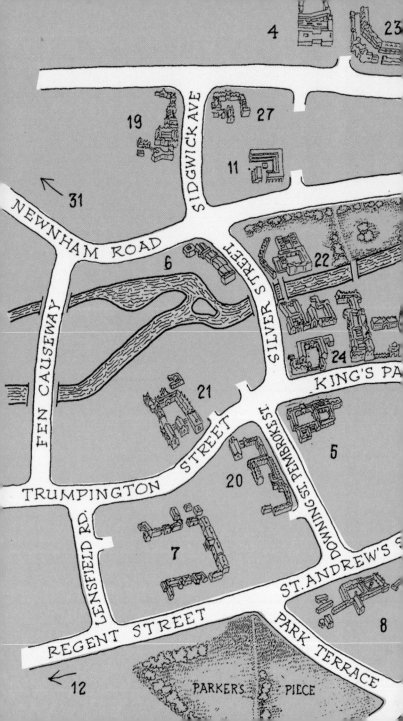